2 by South

Precious Blood
and
Rattlesnake in a Cooler

ONE ACT PLAYS

BY

FRANK SOUTH

RATTLESNAKE PUBLISHING

For permissions, email **rattlesnakepublishing@gmail.com** or write to: Rattlesnake Publishing Inc. 205 Hunters Ridge Rd, Warner Robins, Georgia 31093

2 by South – Precious Blood and Rattlesnake in a Cooler
Both plays revised for this edition   Copyright © 2020 by Frank South
Precious Blood   Copyright © 1981 by Frank South
Rattlesnake in a Cooler   Copyright © 1980 by Frank South

First Edition – September 21, 2020

ISBN: 978-1-7353820-0-5
ISBN: 978-1-7353820-1-2 (Kindle)

Library of Congress Control Number: 2020915345

2 by South first printed and circulated in manuscript form by Plays in Process 1981-82
Theatre Communications Group, Inc. 520 Eighth Ave., 24th Fl, NY, NY 10018-4156

Photo Credits: All photos property of contributors listed. All rights reserved.
Cover photo by Marty Heitner ©Marty Heitner
pgs. 71-72 courtesy of Marty Heitner ©Marty Heitner, pgs. 73-74 courtesy of Richard S. Bailey ©Richard S. Bailey, pgs. 75-76 © Joan Pagliuso, pg. 77 courtesy of Walt Disney Television ©American Broadcasting Companies, Inc., pg. 78 1st photo courtesy of Detroit Repertory Theatre ©Bruce Millan, 2nd photo courtesy of Daniel Burmester, pg. 79 1st photo courtesy of James Horan, 2nd photo courtesy of Mary Gould, pg. 80 Frank South archives.

Excerpt from "Somebody's Daddy" by and courtesy of Daniel D. Darst, Al Galico Music BMI
Excerpt from "The English Teacher" by Lily King   Copyright © 2005 by Lily King

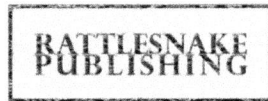

RATTLESNAKE
PUBLISHING

GOOD BOOKS WITH A BITE

rattlesnakepublishing.com
facebook.com/RattlesnakePublishing

TO ROBERT AND KATHRYN ALTMAN

FOR THEIR FRIENDSHIP AND SUPPORT

ALSO BY FRANK SOUTH

A CHICKEN IN THE WIND AND HOW HE GREW
STORIES FROM AN ADHD DAD

ALOHA ISLAND — THE STORY OF THE STONES

PLAYS

PAY ATTENTION

THE NIGHT TALKERS

SWIMMING

CONTENTS

PRECIOUS BLOOD

"Memory does its work underground. Beneath consciousness, a past moment finds its kin all at once. Like a fish returned to its school, it frolics in remembered waters, and stirs up others."

\- Lily King
The English Teacher

This is a play of snarled and buried memories. The characters never directly interact. The audience is the light to which each of them is drawn, to help unearth and slash apart their entwined pasts.

CHARACTERS

UNC – an unassuming middle-aged working man. He enters wearing a raincoat, grey work pants, a tan work shirt over a white t-shirt, and work boots – all well-used. He has a worn robe pre-set on the couch.

CONNIE – an R.N. her 30's. Proud and compassionate, she carries a scar that rests uneasily in her. She sleeps in a loose shorts and chemise. She changes into blue scrubs with a patterned top, a loose red cardigan and white walking shoes for work.

MELODY – a young girl, Unc's niece. Funny, curious, and full of life.

MELODY and CONNIE are to be played by the same actor.

TIME - Present day, a rainy night.

PLACE - Kansas City, Kansas and Sedalia, Missouri

SET – DOWNSTAGE CENTER is a Doctor's waiting room with a settee, end table, and dressing screen.
STAGE RIGHT is a raised kitchen area, in the style of institutions, with window, sink, cupboard below.
DOWNSTAGE LEFT is a raised portion of the living room of a mobile home trailer with a worn sofa and coffee table. A sliding trailer-style window with curtains is above the left arm of the couch.
UPSTAGE CENTER is Connie's raised bedroom area with a door SL at the corner. DSL of the door is a small wall sink in the corner with mirror and towel rack above it. CR of the door a curtained window is centered above Connie's single bed. Next to the head of the bed is a small end table with a reading lamp, book, and alarm clock. A bureau and side chair are against the wall near the foot. A rag doll sits on the bureau.

AT RISE:

> *SOUND of rain. CONNIE is in bed asleep. UNC, in a wet raincoat, enters the bedroom, crosses to the bureau, and picks up the rag doll. CONNIE sits up, turns on a lamp, scans the room, <u>not seeing</u> UNC, who stands, looking at the doll. CONNIE turns the lamp off, goes back to sleep. UNC sits the doll back on the bureau, crosses DSC to the waiting room as LIGHTS FADE UP. UNC sees the audience, takes off his dripping raincoat, hangs it on a hook at the end of the dressing screen, sits on the settee, picks up a magazine from the end table, and flips pages. He glances back to the audience and tosses the magazine back on the table.*

UNC

Kansas. You know, if you drive east across Kansas, miles of land flat as a bed with army corners, as soon as you hit the state line into Missouri, I swear to God the land just bucks up and rolls, and welcomes you in. Kansas is an awful state, burnt and brown. The nicest things about it are the turnpike and the Stuckey's Rest Stops. I'll never understand why my brother moved there to raise his family. Look, a veterinarian can live anywhere, and don't give me that "large animal" shit either, there are cows and horses in every state of the Union. Kansas killed his wife Bucky. She got so bored, she started taking flying lessons in Wichita. First solo flight flipped it over and exploded. Couldn't land the thing worth a damn.

UNC stands and faces the audience. He moves around the stage as he describes the lakes.

My brother Chad and I grew up in the green, hilly countryside of Missouri where our family lived for generations. As a matter of fact, we were all packed into one area of Sedalia. A three mile stretch of road between two lakes, well one was a reservoir with sloping concrete sides which were only there for when the water was extra high. The rest of the time you kind of slid and skedaddled down the side till you got to the tan colored clay lake bottom. From there you could walk around the whole thing, depending on how high the lake was. If it was a little high it could cut you off, what with the trees growing out of the clay and inlets and all. That was Long's Pond.

The other one was smaller, on the opposite side of the highway and down the hill from the houses. It's funny, you could never get to that lake, it was surrounded by marsh, and silty, thick mud. There was no beginning to that lake. You'd walk towards it and it would slowly start to goop up your feet and make sucking sounds when you walked. The reeds up around your armpits and your arms sticking straight out like you were on a tightwire and you'd grab at the reeds, but they couldn't hold you up or help you in any way. You could lose a shoe in there. Forget it, it was too much trouble. Like I told Chad, if you want to go swimming in there so bad and get eaten up by alligators and swallowed by muck go right ahead, but you're stupider than sin.

CONNIE'S alarm goes off. UNC hears it somewhere in the back of his head. CONNIE gets up, turns off the alarm and moves SR to the kitchen to put water on for coffee. UNC continues with his story, oblivious to her.

UNC

I picked that up from my Great Aunt Alma, "stupider that sin."
Doesn't make much sense really. She lived farthest up the
road, right up where the bridge used to be before it got washed
out in a spring flood when I was around five, and the county
never bothered to replace it because Route 2 was just the
bottom part of a horseshoe anyway. You see, the main highway
looped around, and our road led to the same highway it left,
and since there were only eight houses and five families on the
road anyway why bother? Suited us fine. Living on a dead-end
country road was like having your own private estate.

> *UNC sits on the edge of the platform near the trailer.*
> *CONNIE crosses SL to her bedroom to make her bed,*
> *stops, and turns to the audience.*

CONNIE

You know, sometimes a place will fool you. The first Friday I
drove to the trailer the road was beautiful. Wet black asphalt
with all that green right up to the edge of it. It turned, dipped
and then rose to a bluff as it passed between the two lakes. It
stopped at a river. Went right to the edge and stopped.

> *The kettle whistles. CONNIE crosses to the kitchen,*
> *makes a cup of instant coffee, crosses back to sits on*
> *the bedroom chair as UNC crosses SL to the trailer.*

UNC

Great Aunt Alma also invented the family whistle. We'd be
over at her house for dinner and well, it's not actually a house.
When I was born, she decided that it was too crowded in the
family house and put up a mobile home on some land the
family owned by the river. Dad said it was like walking around

UNC (cont.)

in a tin can but really it was an expensive unit. It's a double-wide, which is pretty roomy, with Aunt Alma's old sewing room that I made into an extra bedroom, and when Melody moved in, I put in a half bathroom.

UNC accidentally steps into CONNIE'S bedroom area where she sits on her chair with her coffee. He senses her, but it's his niece, MELODY he feels there, as if she's in the bathroom, and he immediately turns away.

UNC

I mean, I thought for a girl of that age it was only proper. We shouldn't be doing our business on the same toilet.

CONNIE crosses to the kitchen, puts the cup in the sink.

CONNIE

You know, after all this time I still don't like being touched or held. I sleep alone and wonder if the time I spent with Melody and her uncle will stay with me for the rest of my life.

She crosses back to the bedroom, stops and turns to the audience.

When you extend your hand, when you really give, you just lay your heart on the table and hand someone else the hammer. I'll never do that again. I think that makes me a good nurse.

CONNIE changes into her scrubs for work. UNC crosses DC to the audience.

But the thing with the whistle is that when we were kids and out playing before dinner she'd come to our porch and whistle for us to come in when it was time to eat. By that time, she was coming over to make dinner for us every night. Dad was in charge of breakfast; we'd pack our own lunches. This whistle, though, changed all the time, she couldn't keep it straight. Sometimes twoo-wee-oo then the following week twee-twee-wee-oo, or twoo-woo-wee-oo, like the beginning of the song Dad said was the one she had shared and sung with her old beau. Dad said that when she was a girl, she and her boyfriend used to go swimming a lot, and once Alma dove off the bridge on a dare when the water was too low and broke her back.

WHAP - A newspaper is delivered, banging against the bedroom door. CONNIE picks up the paper and reads as UNC continues.

It took her a long time to recover and I guess her boyfriend got tired of waiting around, so he married someone else and left town.

UNC crosses SL to the couch in the trailer and sits.

She never much bothered with men after that and devoted herself to helping raise Chad and me and being the school nurse. I tell you, that was one pain in the neck; you could never get off sick from school when you were bored or itchy. You had to be practically dead for your own Great Aunt to send you home. No matter what the whistle, though, we'd almost always get our tails back to the house as soon as we heard her. She looked a sight too, as we'd be running toward her. She'd be standing on this mid-western porch with her slacks on, and

UNC (cont.)

her cigarette in a holder. I bet she was the only woman in Sedalia who used a cigarette holder. Chad said she looked just like Katherine Hepburn. I didn't know who that was exactly, I was around nine and he was in his early teens, so he knew more than I did. He said she was an old-time movie actress who wore pants and pushed people around.

CONNIE crosses to the bathroom sink and begins washing her face.

I wondered if she hugged people as much as our Aunt Alma hugged us, or rather, Chad. I think Chad got more attention that I did, not from Mom and Dad. Nobody got any attention from Mom.

UNC stands and crosses DSC.

When she'd come downstairs for a while to sit with the family after dinner - she always ate up in her room, sometimes with Dad, but mostly alone - she'd look at each of us closely for a second, never touching. I remember thinking for a long time that she was checking to see if we had washed our faces. Then she'd sit back a bit, smoking her Salems, digging the fingernail of her forefinger into the cuticle of her thumb, and stare out the window at the marsh lake. Her thumbs were always bleeding where she would dig at them, and when Dad or Aunt Alma would put band-aids on them she'd dig through those so her thumbs looked frayed and thick.

UNC crosses back to the couch and sits and leans back.

Dad was nice enough to us, but he spent most of his time and attention on Mom or his shooting friends. He'd ruffle our hair and tell us neat things, like how one of our great-great grandfathers had been a rebel cavalryman at Shiloh. Or how our grandfather had owned almost all of the land around Sedalia and had once turned down being Governor - oh, a whole load of shit. Basically, he was a walking World Book about himself and our whole fancy dead family.

> *UNC lies down on the couch, closes his eyes, and sleeps. CONNIE dries her face with a towel.*

CONNIE

When Melody was nine years old, she had a fight with her father, and she said -

> *When MELODY speaks, CONNIE becomes wholly the free and awkward girl that haunts her.*

MELODY

Look buddy, you may be my father and all, and I know you're a big man and all, but if I really want to go camping with Billy Saracino, there's nothing you can do to stop me. Lock me in my room, I'll escape out the window. Lock the windows, set the alarms, and tie me to a chair, I'll kill myself while you and Mom are asleep. I'll wiggle free, sneak into your study and steal the Bowie knife you got from the mayor and cut the veins in my throat, and you'll find me in the morning lying there in the middle of a pool of sticky red blood, and I won't even have left you a note. Jeeze, I remember that so clearly, him sitting on the couch and me running back and forth between the kitchen and the living room, throwing myself against anything around. Sometimes I hated him so much. He was so damn proper and sure. He'd take me to get my hair trimmed, he always took me to the barber shop in Wichita, never the beauty parlor. That's where Mom went and would spend all afternoon. I never went in there but once that I can remember, and that spray and color and smell made me feel caught. Like I was going to get all glued up, like those flies on those long yellow tapes in the garage or something.

But when Dad would walk with me, people would nod at him and pat my head and kind of push me along, and say 'Hello, Chad,' 'How you doin', Chad,' 'How's it goin', Chad?' They all liked him so much. He and his friends seemed to coo at each other. The same way Mom and her friends would cluck back and forth when they'd come over to the house for whatever. Cookies and bourbon, I think.

> *MELODY crosses USL, picks up the doll from the bureau, throws herself onto the bed, and plays with the doll as she talks.*

But they never made those comfort sounds to each other. At home they screeched like crows, sometimes late into the night. Even before I knew anything about sex and kids and all, I knew I'd never have a brother or sister. There was no reason, they'd used up any happiness they had to make me. There was no room for anyone else. In a way, that had to make you feel special.

> *MELODY leaves the doll on the bed, crosses DSC to the magazines, picks one up, flips through.*

MELODY (cont.)
I guess I only hated Dad when he'd say no in that way that you
knew that there was no way out. No matter what you did he'd
shake his head sitting there on the couch with all these papers
and books in his lap, hardly even looking at you. You knew he
was just thinking about hogs and sheep and cows and what
made them sick. Mom read paperbacks or watched TV in their
bedroom and would ruffle your hair without looking at you
and say ask your dad. And he'd already said no, so you wanted
to break all the windows and kill them both.

> *MELODY slams the magazine down, and stomps back*
> *USL to the bedroom and puts on the robe.*

'Course later when they were dead, you could give a hoot about
Billy Saracino. Even then I loved my father most because I
hated him most because he cared enough to at least have an
opinion. About me, I mean. The only opinion my mother
seemed to have was how she thought black people over-ran the
Greyhound busses in the summer, so she didn't feel safe
sending me up to see her mother for part of vacation. "Those
Greyhounds are getting darker and darker," she'd say. Then
Dad would call her an ignorant racist, which she was, no
doubt, and she'd call him a selfish son of a bitch who didn't
care about anybody but himself, which wasn't true at all, and
they'd go screeching on into the night.

> *CONNIE is back. She stands up and makes the bed.*

CONNIE
Imagine her having the guts to be that honest with me. Melody
was eleven years old when she told me about her mom and
dad. She'd been living with her uncle in Sedalia for two years.

The doll falls off the bed. CONNIE picks it up, and holding it with care, crosses to the chair and sits.

Not quite two years later, she was dead.

UNC hums a child's song. He sits up, facing the audience.

UNC

But I do think Great Aunt Alma really favored Chad. Now I'm not sure and I'm not even sure that it matters, except that Mom kind of passed him along personally to Aunt Alma, stared at him longer in the after-dinner family times, or maybe it was just that one time.

CONNIE, sitting on the chair holding the doll, straightens its hair, smooths its dress, lost in memory. UNC sees her, but it's the image of his mother and Chad he sees. He turns away.

I don't know, maybe I dreamed this, but I remember when I was real little, the bathroom door was open a little, and Mom was sitting on the edge of the bathtub with her clothes on and all, crying and holding Chad, squeezing him, her fingers digging into his shoulders, saying you're my only little boy, you'll always be my only little boy and crying all the more. Thing was, Chad's pants were down. I think he just wanted to go to the bathroom. He was probably holding it all the time this was going on. Kind of funny when you think about it.

He sits on settee and picks up a magazine again. He makes two pop sounds using his mouth and finger. CONNIE hears, puts the doll back on the bureau and looks out her bedroom window.

UNC

Every Sunday, weather permitting, you'd hear them down at the marsh lake shooting skeet, Dad and his friends. Sometimes you'd hear their voices yelling "Draw!" But that was real faint. Mostly what you heard was this echoey pop-corn popper way down in the haze. In duck season they'd take Mr. Feasel's dogs with them and you wouldn't hear a sound until the squawking of some stupid mallards scouting out the marsh, and then the whole lake would kind of explode at once and a bunch of the birds would plop into the lake, like deposits.

UNC drops the magazine on the end table.

It was during the skeet shooting time that Dad tripped while holding his shot-gun wrong and blew out his stomach.

UNC makes the <u>pop sound</u> *again.*

One of those pops down there was him.

CONNIE shrugs off whatever she heard and puts on her shoes for work. UNC snorts at his joke, then continues.

Then there was yelling and cars squealing, and Mom quickly lost the rest of her marbles and got packed off to a nursing home of some kind. Later they moved her to the state hospital in Fulton. That's the only place I ever visited her. Still do, once in a while.

UNC picks up a magazine again and starts reading. CONNIE slips on her red cardigan and crosses downstage to the audience.

CONNIE

Look, I've been doing things for people for as long as I can remember, that's just the way I operate. I don't think that there is anything particularly good about it, it's simply my habitual subservience. I was a candy striper in high school and during college I started with the Big Sister program. That's how I met Melody and her uncle. I guess she had been living with him for about six months in this little backwater, but pretty part of Missouri, north of Sedalia, when I started seeing her twice a week. Friday afternoons when she got off school and almost all-day Sunday.

> *CONNIE crosses DSL. In describing her clothes, she looks into an imaginary mirror. UNC sits right on the other side of her mirror. UNC looks away and pulls some candy pieces out of his shirt pocket.*

I was wearing the closest thing I had to a suit at the time when I went to meet them. Really, it wasn't a suit at all, a kind of nice brown corduroy skirt, a brown tweed jacket past it's day, and a white blouse that buttoned to the neck. I don't know why a person, when they're trying to feel secure and impress someone, would wear a skirt. It's respectable and all, but your legs are so out there like on a shelf to be looked at, and why? For Christ's sake, why?

But I'm jumping ahead and judging myself again, but Nuns should wear pants if anybody should, don't you think? Ah, but that's just crap anyway you should be able to walk around naked if you want to without worrying that some evil asshole is going to jump on you from out of nowhere and try and shove himself inside of you and beat the living shit out of you in the bargain.

CONNIE (cont.)
But meeting Melody and her uncle for the first time was surprisingly easy.

She crosses over to the trailer area.

Imagine yourself walking up the wooden steps to a trailer in a place you've never been before. I was going to school in Sedalia, but I didn't know much about the areas around the town, where you'd go for Sunday drives and see the country. Anyway, I knocked on the aluminum door and went into a strange living room to offer myself as a personal friend to people I'd never met. I had done this kind of thing before and there was always room for suspicion and sort of a false sense of decorum, so guarded, unready to be seen. A family for the most part does not want its belly exposed.

> *CONNIE slips off her cardigan and jumps onto the couch next to UNC, <u>acting as MELODY but speaking as CONNIE</u>. Here, all three worlds brush closely. She takes the candy from UNC's hand and eats it.*

But these two were like a couple of people off The Hollywood Squares. Full of in-jokes and camaraderie, and ready to tell me anything about them or anything else. We ate hot ham sandwiches on white bread with mustard, drank cokes and laughed a lot.

> *UNC glances at his empty hand, then stands and crosses to the kitchen to do repairs. CONNIE spits out the candy, laughs and falls into MELODY completely. She grabs a couple of magazines and crawls to the settee center stage, which becomes her root house.*

MELODY

Come on, you gotta crawl on your knees, come on its just clay besides its nice in here once you get in. I bet I'm the only person in the world with a root house, everybody's got a treehouse, but I'm the only one with a house underneath a tree. Course when the lake gets higher, I'll get washed out. But see? I made a floor with this old piece of linoleum. Unc had it rolled up underneath the sink. I think he was going to throw it away, so I took it, looks just like the kitchen at home doesn't it? And if you lift up this corner here, that's my safe where I keep things. I've got some rocks and stuff, but best is this magazine I took from Unc's closet.

MELODY holds a girlie magazine she grabbed from the end table.

Are my breasts going to end up like this? I mean I've already got some hair and all but when do you know when your breasts are finished? Yours are kind of big, not as big as hers, but will yours keep going or did they stop already? Mine are starting to kind of be there but I don't know if they're done yet. Do you think I'm too old to be crawling around in the dirt like this? I guess I should start to learn about dresses and doing my hair and all, but I think I'd rather be a zoologist. I think I like animals the way my Dad did, I think I got that from him.

UNC turns from sink, points a caulking gun at audience.

UNC

I was the one who was supposed to have been the veterinarian, not Chad. I was the one who cried when Lassie was about to drown in the river because the current was too strong.

MELODY

I've got this National Geographic here too. I should probably take that with me today in case the lake rises in the night. It's a reservoir you know, and they can fill it anytime they want. This is the time of year they seem to fill it the most too. Last night I was lying in bed and I kept on thinking that the water was seeping into my root house and I couldn't come down here in the dark to get my National Geographic. But look at this lady. She knows a whole lot about lions, she lives with them in Africa. I think I'd like to work with her. See? She doesn't have to tease her hair or show her breasts or anything. I think I'd be a good zoologist though. Unc wants me to start dressing up soon, I think. Last time he said we should go shopping in the Junior Miss section at JCPenney, I told him to stuff it.

Back as CONNIE, she stands, crosses to the trailer, picks up her cardigan, slips it on, crosses to the settee.

CONNIE

She always wore her hair in a ponytail. I remember it swinging back and forth when she ran ahead of me. She beat me in every foot race we ever had.

UNC sits next to CONNIE on the settee, pulls out a sandwich from brown paper bag. Here, Unc and Connie's worlds brush closely, unaware but familiar.

UNC

Every Sunday Great Aunt Alma would set us up with TV trays, sandwiches and soda and we'd watch Lassie, Walt Disney and Bonanza. Chad just laughed and sang at me, "Lassie's too smart, now she's floating in the water Lassie's too smart now

UNC (cont.)

she's croaking in the water Lassie's too smart now she's bloating in the water and you'll cry till you throw up."

Most of the time, though, Chad and I were like a team when we played. He was the leader, but we were always together. But once I remember there was this girl that Chad had met at school who lived on our Route, but closer to where the highway still connected, and somehow she ended up with us when we were going to goof around Longs Pond.

UNC stands up and crouches a bit re-enacting what happened, creeping around the screen.

We were playing Civil War scouts which we played a lot anyhow. looking for Union soldiers and stuff, but this time we'd only been out for a little bit when they told me they were Union spies and they tied me to a tree. I even told them I was a Union Spy too, but they said they didn't believe me and left. It took me about an hour to get free and by then I was too cold and tired to go look for them. I just went home.

UNC crosses to the trailer and sits on the couch.

Chad came home later, I think it was even dark outside, and he didn't say anything about it, but from then on, he began telling me a lot about girls.

UNC lies face down, hugging a pillow to his chest.

"It's the neck, once you kiss them on the neck, they really start to give you stuff. The tongue, get that tongue in there and really move it around, cause then their hips start to move the same

24

way. Bucky won't let me do anything but play with her boobs, but I've been getting my knee in there and working between her legs. She already rubs me till I let go, and even unzips me and holds me in her hand and squeezes when I tell her to. Ha. I'll get her this summer for sure, boy."

UNC stands and crosses downstage to the audience.

He doesn't get her that summer, but he gets a bunch of others, summer after summer, and he tells me every second of it, too – every second. But Bucky never lets him get much past second base, no matter what he tries. I asked Chad why he called her that – Bucky. Her name was Carol. She first told Chad that she got the nickname because she was rebellious growing up, like a bucking bronco. But later, she said really it was sort of code for buxom, because she developed early and had such big, um, you know, breasts. Her dad was the one who came up with it. Bucky was the one he married, though. So, if that's what she was after, I guess she played him just right. Melody was born after they'd been married about a year.

UNC crosses up to the chair in the bedroom and sits. CONNIE stands at the kitchen sink, cleaning up.

See, Chad you went off and Great Aunt Alma and I started our own life together and closed off part of the old house. First year I cooked, we talked, and I tucked her into bed, until finally one morning she didn't feel like getting up and a week later she passed away. It's alright, don't worry, I can take care of the details. No, I know you're swamped right now, she wouldn't blame you for not coming. She wasn't much of one for ceremony.

She did touch my face though, a couple of mornings before she died. "You're a strange one, a male Cinderella, waiting for the Ball, scrubbing and working. Well kiddo, there's nothing left to scrub. So, you better skedaddle on out of here and start over like your brother did."

> *CONNIE crosses DSL in front of UNC to pick up the paper sandwich bag UNC left by the settee. UNC sees her as Great Aunt Alma. When CONNIE crosses back USR to the kitchen UNC jumps up from the chair and crosses to the kitchen to confront her.*

Listen - I can build a kitchen better than anybody. I'm an honest salesman and I know my products. That damn sure counts for something.

> *CONNIE doesn't respond. UNC ricochets off her to cross DSC to the audience.*

Go ahead, ask me anything about Kitchen Aid, GE, Westinghouse - even French products, Cuisinart or Superior. Hitachi has just put out a dishwasher, I bet you didn't know that. Piece of junk too, no better than a Magic Chef. I can install roll-top Formica quicker, cleaner, and cheaper than anybody in Missouri. And shit, I'm alive. That is something to say for this family. It's like we all just lined up and walked into a combine. I'm the only one that had enough sense to take a detour.

> *He sits at the settee. CONNIE crosses to the settee and stands for a beat, then transforms into MELODY and she sits on floor near his legs.*

UNC (cont.)

After Bucky flipped her plane over, I went to Wichita to stay with Chad and Melody for a couple of weeks. Melody and I got along fine.

UNC pats MELODY'S head.

Afternoons, we went to the bowling alley near Chad's office. I made the meals, and sometimes Melody and I would just stay in the house, eat toaster pizza, and watch the soaps. Sometimes we'd just play gin rummy all afternoon.

MELODY casually rests her arm on her uncle's knee.

But my brother Chad kept bumping into things when he was home, never would sleep in his and Bucky's bedroom, always on the couch. I slept in their bed. I didn't get much sleep either.

UNC gently removes MELODY'S arm from his knee and crosses DSC. MELODY eavesdrops on UNC'S story.

You know how my brother died? There's this machine, it's called a bull- extractor. It's like a milking machine for getting semen for artificial insemination. Well, when you hook one of these things on a big Holstein bull you got to have him held pretty secure in this metal gate contraption cause he tends to become pretty excited and move around a lot. Chad would go around and be in on these projects occasionally, especially if it was a champion like this one, to make sure his patients were being taken care of right.

UNC (cont.)

The machine was on and Chad noticed the side latch of the pen was working loose and he crouched down by the side gate to secure it and when he pushed down it snapped off in his hand, and the bull's hip hit that side, the gate broke and swung open, catching Chad on the chin, laying him on his back, and the bull's hooves, kicking free now, came down on, and pretty much went through his chest.

MELODY breaks and runs USL to the bed as if hearing this for the first time. UNC crosses back to the trailer, takes off his shoes and shirt, puts on his robe, closes the curtain and lies down on the couch.

That was in the second week of my stay. I stayed an extra week to put Chad in the ground and took Melody home with me. Right before we left, I went by the cemetery with some plastic lilies for Chad's grave. I wanted something that would last because I didn't intend to ever come back. But they only allowed real flowers. I threw them out the window when we drove out of there. Melody just stared at the dashboard as we left flat, dry Kansas and drove into the green hills of Missouri.

CONNIE stands next to the bed holding the doll. She puts it down on the bed, crosses DSC to the audience.

CONNIE

She was afraid of the dark. Simple enough, she was a kid. But it was the smell of it that woke her up. I stayed over a couple of Friday nights, when the weather was bad and my little Toyota would have slid off the road in the dark, and I'd see the light go on in her little room then off, then on in her bathroom, then

CONNIE (cont.)
off. Then I'd hear her feet padding across the trailer to where I lay on the living room couch.

She crosses SL of the settee where UNC'S raincoat is hanging. UNC is breathing audibly in his sleep, and she falls into MELODY.

MELODY
It's that wet marshy smell that clogs you up so you can't breathe. I've noticed ever since I moved here with Unc. It's only at night after Unc goes to sleep, and the smell's just faint in the air, just a little more than during the day.

Wind blows the door open. UNC gets up, crosses USL, closes the door and walks into the bedroom, looks down at the doll.

But just when I'm about ready to fall asleep, just on the edge where everything seems safe, there's this smell like something breathing the marsh smell, is getting bigger or closer. I only screamed once, and when Unc came in I screamed and cried some more because the light was off, and I thought it was him.

UNC picks up a pillow from the floor, slowly puts the pillow behind the doll's head, and props her up.

I always think the marsh guy's hands are big like pillows that will go over your face so you can't scream.

UNC crosses DSR to the kitchen and pours himself a glass of milk. MELODY crosses USL to the bedroom.

MELODY

Once when Unc came to meet me where the school bus lets me off, he said he hated the marsh lake too. But I never really told him about the marsh breathing guy, and I don't think that place scares him as much as it does me. I like Long's Pond though. and this trailer. And Unc's great, so that's something. Unc should be around more though. I was real glad when he called up the Big Sister program, I tell you. I saw the ad on TV and asked him and he called up the next day, just like that. You've worked out real good too. I mean Unc spends a lot of time out on the job, tearing out people's kitchens and stuff, and when he comes home, he spends a couple of hours in his bedroom with the door closed. When he's around he's real nice, and funny. Don't you think he's funny?

UNC finishes his milk and crosses DSL to the trailer, passing in front of MELODY on the bed.

Sometimes he'll come out of his room on Saturday when he's supposed to make a real breakfast and all, with his boxer shorts on and one of those funny t-shirts with the kind of straps instead of sleeves, and his hands will be over his head like a ballet dancer, and he'll prance around the living room yelling that he's the goddess of spring, and this little puppy we had for a while, Buzzer, is yapping and falling down and trying to bite his ankles and he keeps yelling that he's the goddess of spring and you can't hurt the goddess of spring. I think I laughed harder at that than I've laughed at anything in my whole life. You know what his favorite movie is? "Lady and the Tramp," even though he doesn't like dogs that much. Guess that's why Buzzer ran off.

Back as CONNIE, she crosses DSC to the audience.

CONNIE

For April Fool she snuck into his bedroom and put a whole tube of toothpaste in his shoes. Only she did it on his birthday in March because she figured he'd be looking for it in April.

CONNIE crosses USL to the bed, gets in and turns the light off. UNC sleeps on the couch. The stage is dark. UNC's breathing is audible again. Then he wakes.

UNC

At first, I thought it was a dream. Any way I moved my head I couldn't breathe, and I couldn't move my arms, then I heard his voice and I was awake. "Don't scream don't move I've got a knife at your throat."

UNC sits up. Re-living this, he feels the intruder behind him. UNC stands, crosses USR to the kitchen and around USL to the bedroom. As if the intruder holds him, UNC'S head is pulled back, the knife at his throat.

"You sit up real slowly, that's right, now we're going to hold this bag and put any money or anything valuable you got in it while I hold this knife right on your jugular and hold your hair real tight like this, so let's take a little tour."

We got my wallet, Aunt Alma's ring and bracelet, the kitchen money for extras and Melody's lunch at school, and then we started moving towards the living room and I told him I didn't keep anything of value there just matches and magazines on the coffee table and stuff. But he pulled my head back a little tighter and pushed me forward and Melody yelled. And her light went on.

UNC falls to his knees. CONNIE'S bedroom light goes on and she jumps up, looking at the doll on her bed and then at the audience.

CONNIE

When I found them, Melody was all curled up like a baby in a womb, or somebody playing hide-n-go-seek and trying to be extra quiet. And her uncle was making babbling sounds and was sweating all over sitting on the floor, next to the bed, his back against the wall, his hands all red, and it looked like holding his guts in. It turns out it wasn't that bad of a cut.

UNC stands, crosses DSC, and faces the audience.

UNC

"Who's that?" And I said just a kid and he says OK let's see, and I say no, I got some more money in the kitchen I didn't show you, he says let's see the kid, and he makes me open the door and Melody screams again, and he says shut her up. And, and I say it's alright Melody it's just Unc, and she says who's he, who's he? And I say just a man who wants things.

And he says, "Hey that's no kid, come here honey, you holding out the big prize for last, mister. Okay, lay down buddy, near the wall right next to your little honeypot. That's fine, now face the wall. That's right."

Melody is hyperventilating and making gobbling kind of sounds and crawling to the corner near the wall by my head and I can feel him grab her and pull her down, and I start to move and he says, "I got the knife against her belly just like it was against your neck. You move again and I'll give her another hole."

UNC (cont.)
I start yelling, "It's a dream, Melody it's a dream, you're dreaming really dreaming!" She's just making sounds and he says he wants her to hold it then he'll give it to her and can't stand it and I scream and throw myself over on him and pull him off, and Melody screams. He hits me with the butt of the knife I think, and Melody screams again. I forget anything else.

UNC sits on settee. CONNIE gets ready for work.

CONNIE
She was dead, of course. He was left for dead, I guess. Jesus, I hear stories. You wouldn't believe the shit I hear. I've been an R.N. at the University of Kansas Medical Center in Kansas City, Kansas, three blocks from the Missouri state line, for a couple of years now. I work the Emergency Room from three in the afternoon until eleven at night.

CONNIE crosses DSR.

You can hear the scream of the siren minutes before the ambulance pulls up to the automatic doors and somebody gets pushed in on a cart dead or dying or just butchered and abused.

CONNIE crosses to the trailer.

CONNIE
Melody and her uncle are five, almost six years ago in my life, but I guess there are things in everybody's life that they can't shake. Like that trailer on that dead-end country road.

CONNIE opens the trailer curtains.

CONNIE (cont.)

Two weeks after the incident, I drove over to meet him at the trailer, to help him pack the last of his things. He was selling the last of the family property and moving into a hotel-apartment in Sedalia. I hugged him.

UNC stands from the settee, crosses to the trailer, CONNIE reaches out to hug him. He walks by her and turns to the audience

UNC

I bet you my mother was raped.

UNC crosses DSC to the settee and sits.

I bet that's why she looked at us so close, to see which one was real, what the difference was. I bet you that's what happened. No wonder she went nuts, seeing her rapist growing up around her, seeing him all over again. But she couldn't be sure. Maybe she was pregnant at the time and didn't know it, maybe I was really one of theirs. She pretty much just stares at her hands and whistles these soft little songs, like kid's songs, when I visit her these days. Can't get a thing out of her.

CONNIE crosses USL to the bureau to gather what she needs for work.

CONNIE

You do hear a lot of rape stories in my job. You know how a restaurant gets a rush? Well, we get them too. All of a sudden, you're flooded with hurt people and crying kids. But I always know a rape victim. I gravitate towards them when they come in, and you hear it. Over and over again.

CONNIES (cont.)

"I had forgotten to lock the window, I fell asleep watching TV, he had a knife and he stayed for two and a half hours; he couldn't come."

CONNIE crosses DSC to the audience.

"After the guy chased me into the bar, just this guy on the street, he had all this makeup on. These two cops beat him up and one took him to jail and the other cop took me home. That cop made sure that I got into my apartment safe, then followed me in and took me, like I was Kleenex or a picture in a magazine. He told me his name, for Christ's sake. No, I don't remember. I can't tell you, forget it."

CONNIE crosses to the trailer and hugs the air again.

I hugged him. He wasn't crying but he was tense and a little shaky. There wasn't a lot in the way of furniture left, some boxes filled with pots and pans, an overstuffed chair, the dining room table, and two chairs. He was drinking tall glasses of gin and lime juice. There was no sign of Melody's things.

CONNIE paces back and forth in the trailer, as the memory takes hold. UNC sits on the settee, staring forward.

He said he wasn't strong, I told him he was. He said it was his fault, I told him it wasn't. He said he understood something now, that he had never been a man, because he was so ashamed of what men did or wanted, like his brother telling him fucking stories every night in the dark of their room.

CONNIE (cont.)

But hey, there was nothing to be ashamed of, right? It was natural, we were all animals and he was tired of pretending he wasn't. Don't want to hold hands and bury people anymore, he said. He wanted what everybody else wanted, and he bet I wanted it too. It'd be a perfect goodbye to the trailer.

CONNIE'S hand rips her uniform as if it was his hand. She re-lives the attempted rape fully, throwing herself onto the couch and to the floor, her hands alternately tearing at herself and defending herself, terrified and enraged.

He always liked my breasts he said. He moved to cut off my exit 'cause I was edging toward the door, and he said it's not like we don't know each other, and it'd help him. And I said take a breath and think about what you're doing. He said, "Come on, you've been around, I haven't, you could show me stuff." He kind of giggled and started to push me back toward the chair and he said some filth and when he said there'd be cum coming out of my ears, I slapped and scratched and bit and he hit, but I ducked and hit him in the stomach where I remembered his cut was.

Gasping for air and control, she scrambles to her feet.

He doubled up and I ran out the door, got in my car, and drove away as fast as I could.

CONNIE dashes out the door, UNC up and right behind her. She slams the door shut, and he runs into it. Pulling himself together, UNC crosses DS to the trailer and the audience.

UNC

I always wondered about Great Aunt Alma's old beau. I bet he
was tall, you know. Thin and elegant sort of, maybe not
elegant, but controlled and at ease. Probably had a lot of girls,
too. In a town like Sedalia, he'd be quite a catch. He'd have to
keep his schedule pretty tight. "Sorry, Bernice, I can't go
tonight. I've got other plans. But how's Tuesday afternoon for
you? Fine, I'll give you a ring."

He crosses to the screen, takes his raincoat, puts it on.

"What to do with Alma? Sweet girl, but too possessive. Well,
when we go swimming tomorrow, I'll think about it. We're
swimming in the river and it's fine.

He crosses USL to the bedroom.

But when she gets out, she starts in with, 'I only see you once
or twice a week. When you were first taking me out, we saw
each other almost every day. I don't appreciate that kind of
treatment.' I tell her I don't appreciate that kind of talk. She
says she doesn't understand, and I tell her I'm not ready for
marriage and fear she is. She says, 'Oh jump go off a bridge,'
and I say why don't you, like that one there? She says, 'I bet
you think I can't, I grew up here, that doesn't scare me one bit.'
I tell her, fine, prove it smart aleck, but the water looks pretty
low. She says, 'I've done this all my life.' She dives. Then she
just floated in the river like a drowned puppy."

UNC picks up the doll from the bed.

He fished her out. Her back was broken. He took her to the
hospital and married Bernice.

UNC hums a waltz, dances with the doll, then props her on the bed with a pillow, and sits in the chair.

UNC

There. Doesn't she look pretty, sitting up straight in her place like that?

CONNIE enters through the bedroom door, crosses DSC.

CONNIE

Even at sixty miles per hour that tree stuck out and I saw it, where Melody's root house had been. Then I was past Long's Pond. I wasn't going to stop for anything, and I was never going to drive down this highway again.

CONNIE crosses USL to the bedroom, takes off her cardigan and throws it across the bed.

I hope Melody believed her uncle and thought it was a nightmare, and that guy was a monster, not a human being. I hope she died thinking that.

She takes off her watch, sets it on the bureau.

I hope. I hope. Every day I hope he doesn't try it again on someone else. I didn't report him, I couldn't, I don't know why. What happened to him doesn't change what he did. But I don't know, I couldn't. It's been six years, and maybe it was my fault somehow. Oh hell no. This is stupid. I sound like I haven't heard years of the shattered cries of rape victims, held them, known them. I will not make excuses for him, that's done. None of this was my fault. And I know one more thing.

CONNIE gets in bed.

I should have turned that bastard in.

She turns out the light. It's dark except for a flash or two of lightning. Rain starts again. UNC stands from the chair, walks by the bed and out the door, closing it behind him.

BLACKOUT

CURTAIN

Rattlesnake in a Cooler

Don't you know you're looking at somebody's daddy?
Or at least he is his mother's son
A hundred years ago he was a hero
Born when he was needed by someone
His way of life had reason and a meaning
And the world had a place for restless men
But now he's like a ship in a bottle
His soul is hungry for a gentle wind

Somebody's Daddy
Daniel D. Darst
Al Gallico Music / BMI

CHARACTERS

DOC – A man in his mid-twenties to late thirties, trying to figure out how he got here and who the hell he really is. The audience is his sounding board and confidant.

Although written to be performed as a monologue by one actor, "Rattlesnake in a Cooler" has also been performed with additional actors added to play Ellen, Jim, and a few other characters in the story without altering the text.

TIME - Present Day

PLACE - A room in Utah

THE SET – An approximately fifteen-foot square cell with slatted wood or bars forming three walls and a ceiling with an open light shaft visible. UPSTAGE RIGHT is a door that leads to a stairway that goes up STAGE RIGHT to STAGE LEFT behind the UPSTAGE wall. The stairway is only seen through the wall slats in the final moments of the play. Preset out of sight directly above the ceiling shaft is a dummy dressed identically as DOC.
UPSTAGE CENTER is a small table and old wooden chair. On the table a half-empty bottle of bourbon sits next to a tin cup.
STAGE LEFT is a wooden cot and bedroll.

MUSIC
The original songs "Somebody's Daddy," "Rough Rider," and "Lonely Man" were used for the opening and closing sequences of the play in the Off-Broadway production and were composed and sung by Danny Darst.
For CDs and info: **dannydarst.com** For rights: Al Galico Music, BMI

"Gold Watch and Chain" is a traditional song in the public domain.

AT RISE –

*Mid-day light streams in through the shaft in the ceiling. DOC
sits on the cot, staring at the floor. He's dressed in dusty
jeans, beat-up cowboy boots and a torn cowboy shirt. He
holds a straw cowboy hat. He lifts his head up, looks at the
audience for a beat, takes a breath, then starts in.*

DOC

When I think about it, Ellen and Jim could've been fucking
twins. Mean tempers inside good people. Or at least that's true
of Ellen. Jim can defend himself. But boy, how Ellen could
break my balls.

"Why don't you take a flying fuck to Pissville, Oklahoma?
Maybe there, God will pay you to sit on your lazy ass and listen
to your tired-ass old country-western albums the whole day
long. I mean, never mind about the goddamned cracked
ceiling in the kitchen that leaks plaster into everything I cook.
If you like little white chips in your snap beans, fine - I'll go out
into the garden and collect ticks all over my legs so we can end
up with lead poisoning like those people in Cleveland."

She tended to become inaccurate when she became excited.
I've told her as much. You can't get lead poisoning from
plaster, only from paint, oil-based paint at that. Although I
had been painting over the crack when it was smaller instead
of actually fixing it, and maybe she remembered and was a

step ahead of me again, but that was month before. It was surely all plaster. Of course, maybe it was lead poisoning that was causing the troubles, though what was eating at me didn't fit the symptoms.

"For Christ's sake, you're a doctor. When you work, the best doc I've seen. What else do you want? My brother's a part-time farmer and a full-time miner and he's happy. Jesus. And Jesse Rollins, up the road, has been harvesting tobacco with one arm and a half-wit son for the last ten years and you don't see him mooning around the backyard with his hands in his pockets humming outlaw ballads and staring at the trees. No, he works, they work, everyone works except for bums and debutantes, that's what puts the frame around life and the family. That's what can heal that empty part you moan about, if you'd just get to it."

> *DOC's up and moving, energized by the memory of the argument. Throughout the rest of the play he's all over the cramped space, sitting – standing – kneeling - drinking, as he re-lives events and the people in them.*

Inaccurate again. Old Jesse couldn't very well put his hands in his pockets, only having one, and you wouldn't find him with that one put away anywhere. When you've only got one, you want it out there where you can use it and people can see how handy it is. But that's it, she's right, they work, but against odds, they fight a fight, I mean getting that crop in is difficult for Jesse what with his son drooling and forgetting what he's doing half the time. And Bill Tarfelt, closer to town, nice piece of land, not too far down in the valley, but four years ago, when everyone else was turning in bumpers of tobacco, his never grown for nothin', dried up halfway through the summer. So he figured too much drainage, maybe an outcrop of lime underneath his land, so he tried grazing, but half his herd died in a freak fever that ran through the county, so he sold what was left, got a loan from the bank using god knows what as collateral, and put up eight chicken shacks and bought a truckload of birds, and a year later put up five more shacks. Seems that land was just meant for pecking and scratching. Now Bill's doing just fine except that last Spring his wife left him for a revivalist from Herpville. But that's just it, you see? Bill has always had bad luck, probably always will, that's what he fights.

But my road was all planned out and smoothed for me, had been for as long as I could remember, all I had to do was keep walking, stay married, have kids, get wealthy, start to twitch, and get palsy as the walls closed in. So, I stopped that life, got off that road, and headed out on my own. I don't care if I was right or wrong or what the results were, it doesn't matter. At least once I moved under my own steam and felt the pressure of one life pushing against another.

I guess I just always wanted to feel definite, unforgiving, and male. Or maybe I just always wanted to be a killer. I don't even know if I married Ellen just to leave her. I did leave her. I did go out west.

There's something stark and solid about the west. Its cleanliness. There's something washed out, removed. There is something in day to day living elsewhere that doesn't exist in Colorado, Utah, or New Mexico. Whatever it is that's missing, its absence makes things better for me.

DOC (cont.)

Late afternoon, after the news and an Ovaltine commercial
this guy came on all excited yelling, six shooters blasting in the
background, "Wanted! The Outlaws! Waylon Jennings, Willie
Nelson, and Jessi Colter have busted open the charts and took
over number one on the charts with this breakout album and
hit single 'My Heroes Have Always Been Cowboys.' If you've
got a wild, restless heart or love someone who does, you need
to run out and get Wanted! The Outlaws!"

I guess that's my earliest memory, three or four years old
sitting on the floor in the kitchen listening to the radio with my
mother in Lexington, Kentucky, and jumping out of my skin
scared, excited and yelling at the shooting and yelling coming
from the radio and Mom laughing as she baked oatmeal bread
and Daddy finished dentistry school. Mom bought that album
too, just like WSM told her to. Something in me changed over
the next couple of years. We could never play that album when
Daddy was around, he hated the stuff. But when he was gone,
Mom and I would play those things until we just about wore
them out. We got so we knew all the words and would sing
along, howlin' and whooping and crying about lost love and
the wide-open range, and I knew that I didn't belong in
Kentucky. I was due out in the Great Southwest, and if I didn't
get on it and get out there, what was waiting for me would be
gone.

But first I had to go to grade school. First in Lexington, and
then in Berea, Kentucky when Daddy set up practice there.
John B. Lesher High School in Berea, University of Kentucky
in Lexington, U.K. Medical School, Lexington, Family Practice
residency, also in Lexington. Lexington, Lexington, Lexington.

DOC (cont.)

Ellen Plunket whacked me in the mouth reaching for a Family
Circle at the check-out at the Kroger. I was behind her and she
had forgotten to pick one up and she reached back in a hurry.
Split my lip and we spent the next forty-five minutes getting to
know each other at the U.K. ER. She found out I was a medical
student and I found out she was a nurse at the V.A. Hospital.
Two years later we were married, two years after that I joined
the practice of an old doc, Wilfred Simpson. Middle class, kind
of sedate, but honest as the day is long, and I admired his
work, so we settled in Boonsborough. I started taking patients
and one day this weathered, bright-eyed old guy comes in.

Wait, don't you see how it was all one big slide? I popped out
of my mother's womb and onto a greased track. I didn't have
to do anything; it was all pre-ordained - except for the
afternoons with my mom, Waylon, and the outlaws, and what
I thought I knew back then. But that didn't fit. Then that old
guy comes in with his bad back, cowboy boots, and that smug
worldly-wise smile on his face.

"Glad to see a young man in this area, real glad, we seem to be
mostly older folk around here, or people hurrying up getting
older, Boonsborough is a boring sort of place for a young man,
but this hard-working, righteous little town fits me like wool
socks. But without a few young men like you, who know what
they want and are serious about life, and can bring some new
blood in here, why, we'd just age ourselves into the ground and
the state would build a highway over us. I admire a man like
you, settled and steady. Bet y'all got a garden. Am I right?"

I asked him to take off his shirt, and he kept on talking all
through the exam.

DOC (cont.)

"Shoot, I was married once, loved her hard. Nobody to this day can look me in the eyes the way she did. Something inside her, I don't know what. Treated her like a dog though, dragged her through too many towns always expected her to be there when I turned around. One morning she started slapping the shit out of me while I was still asleep. I bet she had been staring at me a long time before she did that. Before I was fully awake, she had grabbed her bag, jumped in the car and gone. I expect she went back home, and started teaching again, maybe found herself a man like you. If I wasn't so damn curious about the obvious, I'd be a lot better off. Look, a town's a town, a mountain's a mountain, me seeing it ain't going to change it one whit. Still, I had me some wild times along the way, tangled with some scary fellas, scarier women, and downright frightening livestock. Paid a price, though, paid a price. Hey, whoa up with the yakking, huh? Fact is, I'm an old fart and these days I don't know when to shut up. So, about you. How many kids you planning to have? Because let me tell you something, getting old is a lonely business, being young is all you got so you might as well have it running around your feet calling you Daddy so you can appreciate it. So. How many?"

"I don't really know," I said, "We haven't talked about it. You've strained some muscles in your lower back. It's going to hurt some for a month, I'm going to prescribe some muscle relaxers for you. You can't drive while you're taking them, and you need to get a lot of bedrest for the next two weeks."

I felt like I was the old fart in the room – small, grey and empty. "Tell me something, what would you think of a man who chucked being a doctor - all this safe, settled, steady stuff to go out west and be a rodeo cowboy?"

DOC (cont.)

The old man pulled on his shirt, turned around, his smile gone, and looked at me for a solid minute before he answered, "Well, I don't rightly know what I'd think of such a man. Say, listen, the fact that you are the way you are makes men like me make sense. Someone solid has to be around, otherwise what would hold things together? Stick it out son, regret is a hair shirt. And whatever the fuck you do, don't go into the goddamned rodeo."

I was the handyman for a man named Herb Dawson on the Cherokee Dude Ranch, seven miles north of Livermore, in the Colorado Rockies, just one week after I left Kentucky, I owe that to Jim. I owe a whole lot to Jim, I don't think I could ever pay him back. When I first met him, it was Jim and Pat. They were the wranglers on the place, which meant they took the dudes out on trail rides twice a day, took care of the stable and horses, and danced with the ladies on square dance nights. We shared a cabin together, and considering they just knew me as "a drifter from down south with sort of an honest face" as Jim said, they treated me well. I felt young around these guys.

"What part of Kentucky you from, anyway? You been odd-jobbing all your life? Not in trouble with the law, are you? Alright mister, your job around here is to fix what's broke, muck out the stables, and generally sweep up, pick up, and shut up. Don't drink or get rowdy, at least not around here. Wednesday's your day off, you can most likely get a ride into town with Jim or Pat as that's their day too. Also, you gotta glue the tips back on the pool cues, you gotta clean the pool, and every few days you take this here .22 and go over to the dump and shoot skunks, there's too many of them. Hope Jim was right about you and you don't disappoint either of us."

49

Oh, don't you worry, I won't disappoint you, Herb. I've done
my share of that shit.

DOC Sings.

And I'd pawn you my gold watch and chain love and I'd pawn
you my gold wedding ring
And I'd pawn you this heart in my bosom only say that you'll
love me again
The white rose that blooms in the garden it blooms with this
love in my heart
It broke through on the day that I met you it will die on the day
that we part

Sometimes at the oddest times, I hear Ellen's voice. She had a
number of them, but it's the soft one that sweeps in and
brushes the dust around. She sat on the edge of the bed. She
wasn't crying anymore. She was wearing her blue checked
shirt, the one with the rip at the shoulder. "Whatever it is
that's getting at you, we can get at together. I'm from
Kentucky, I don't know anyplace else, but I'll go anywhere with
you, just bury me here. Okay, you don't want a family now.
Fine. You don't want our garden or the dog and cat. You must
have lied a hundred times then, but I'll accept that. Just don't
walk off with your hands in your pockets, put one around my
waist. Here touch me, feel this, it belongs to you. You're no
longer a kid, you're no longer one person. Don't desert me. I'm
too good to throw away."

Well, sure, I don't know, maybe that's all true, that's fine, but I
can't stretch that far. I'll tell you what though, I'm not going to
put on slippers yet and I know that's really what you want, no

matter what you say. I'm not going to do that. I'm, I'm just going to stop loving you, that's all. That's all. Shit.

I'd sit in this old, abandoned pick-up and stick the rifle out where the windshield used to be and wait. The dump was in the middle of a forest, a mile from the ranch, mounds of dirt, cans, old mattresses, making this kind of little mountain range. They had their burrows there, homes and pathways. You'd just sit tight and wait for them to relax and go about their business, while the magpies gawked and spread one wing and then the other. At first, I was just kicking up dust and making noise, I didn't know how to use the scope or how to squeeze the trigger. But after a while and some practice with tin cans, I got me a couple.

One afternoon I walked in and got in that old truck and there was no breeze. It was dead still, and tense, the air was wound tight. The magpies stood on the branches as still as make-believe. No sound. Until the scratching of the one sent out to be shot. He came out of the burrow hole, walked to the nearest mound and stood on his hind legs like a prairie dog. The damn skunks had drawn straws, and it was probably fixed, he's a poor provider or he's just a chicken shit, well he's dead now, but he's starting to move, nope, pop, got the sucker. The magpies are screaming, he's rolling but he's up scrambling for the burrow hole, pull the bolt back get another round in and he's got his bleeding front in but the white ass with the tail up in the air and the little legs scrambling for footing, Jesus, give me footing, and dead on that white and it exploded and disappeared at the same time. The skunks' front door looked like an open wound, and the screeching is even louder, and I'm out of the truck, and the sky is all black and white wings.

DOC (cont.)
Shut up you fucking rubberneckers, two shots up and they're
gone a flock of moral magpies all heading for church, and I'm
heading out fast when I almost trip on what looks like a stone,
and is really three grey rabbits trying to look like a stone. I
stand right over them. Get out of here, no witnesses, and they
don't move - go on, I said split goddammit. I lower the gun,
one round left, right behind one brown eye is one blue-black
muzzle - so run, I won't shoot you if you fucking run. Don't be
so goddamn afraid of me, alright fine, ok, and BAM.

Two rabbits run and one just flops and rolls there, and I run
and stumble the whole mile back. Ride'm cowboy.

"What did you go and shoot the fucking rabbit for? I mean for
Christ's sake, it's not like you were gonna eat it. Look, forget it.
Let's talk about something else. Ok, look at it this way, you're
trigger happy and a little guilt ridden, that's it. Shit, I first saw
a deer when I was fourteen, and I put a slug from a thirty
ought six right through the neck of the prettiest, most peaceful
doe you ever saw. 'Course at least we field-stripped her, took
her home and chopped her up for food. Point is everybody's a
murderer sooner or later. Take it in stride."

Something about Jim. Seems that he could change subjects
before the first thought was out of his mouth. He was just so
damn impatient. "So, listen, let's get out of here. I got an offer
to ride in Cheyenne Frontier Days, I know some people from
Tri- Star Ranch, well, anyway, look, with all this shit we've
been passing back and forth for the last three months I think
you'd like to see it.   We get along alright, and you can help me
by making sure I stay out of trouble. Pat can handle most of

DOC (cont.)
my shit here and they can hire another handyman. Free
transportation, we'll take my Cherokee. Let's pack it up."

Jim and I left the Cherokee Dude Ranch the next day at six
a.m. The mountains are kind of blue at that hour, even the
ones right next to you. We drove for two hours, stopped and
had biscuits and sausage and sausage gravy and eggs over easy
and orange juice and coffee. The rest of the four hours to
Cheyenne were all beer, cigarettes, and silence. The first time I
met Jim was at breakfast. We got talkative after I passed him
some cream. That was at a truck stop in Greely, Colorado. The
first place I got off the bus from Kentucky.

Man, Cheyenne really goes nuts then. I mean Frontier Days is
the central fucking center of the west. Mom would have loved
to have seen that. Filled with fucking cowboys. Every son of a
bitch you run into is a puncher or a wrangler or a rider or a
bleeder or a stinker or a killer. Believe me, I know what I'm
talking about. The bars are hyped-up Dodge City, filled with
high speed, high tech, foul-spirited bar fights.

Jim bulldogged. Did pretty well I think, I'm not sure how they
judge these things, but he made some money. At night we'd go
out drinking. "You know, I don't particularly like being
bumped into like that. Let's hear you say you're sorry. I don't
believe I heard anything, asshole. Go on, do it. Go ahead and
apologize, you little prick."

All I said was "Hey, stop it, alright?" and wham - the two beers
I was picking up went flying across the room and I was
scrambling to get off my hands and knees. And then wham
again and my head kind of went sideways to the left and I slid

DOC (cont.)

into a table of shot glasses and beer bottles and then
everything went quiet.

Jim was holding the guy's wrists up by his face and talking in
this real low voice. I never understood why, but the madder he
got the quieter he talked. "Alright calm down, calm down, you
just stand there, now. Why are you hitting my friend? Are you
some kind of goddamned fool? I ought to kill you, but I won't,
you just stand there at attention until I pick my friend up there
and we walk out that door. Be nice and obedient when I let go,
or you'll never see your Mama again."

Jim let go and was bending over to help me up when the guy
made a move to kick him in the head. In a flash Jim was all
over him and pulled this little piece of steel out of his back
pocket, there were a couple of crunching sounds, the guy
groaned, started to bleed, and we left.

"I tell you buddy, you're supposed to keep me out of trouble,
not get me in it. I've got enough trouble as it is, and look, you
got my courage all bloody."

Turns out that little piece of steel was a Colt pearl handled,
single shot .22 that he kept in his rear pocket and could really
hurt if you got hit with the butt end of it.

"Look, September tenth there's a rodeo in Roswell, New
Mexico, part of the New Mexico State Fair. I know some guys
down there and I know I can get in if I get down there in time
to register, come on, we'll take turns driving and sleeping,
we've got less than two days. Come on, let's go."

We picked up some gin, beer, and cheese nibs, and took off.
The first leg was going 650 miles south on I-25 to
Albuquerque. We made that in fifteen hours, good time, it's an
old Jeep. We stopped in a Skelly Truck Stop there. Jim was
occasionally hitting the steering wheel as he drove and when
we got out of the car to go in the place, he slammed the shit
out of the door.

He ordered four eggs over easy, sausage and toast. I'd been
eating eggs a lot lately and the yolks were beginning to sicken
me, so I ordered a couple of scrambled. When she brought the
stuff, all Jim's eggs had been cooked in one pan. Now, I don't
know how often you eat in diners, but the little round pans
they cook the eggs in are meant for two eggs, so if you put four
in the white all runs to the center and then after he flips them
over, when you cut into them it's like clear protoplasm on your
plate. That's what happened to Jim. He sent them back, and
through the pass-through you could see this greasy faced cook
snap at the waitress. "If he knew what he wanted he'd get it, if
he wants them over hard, I'll give 'em to him over hard."

Jim's coffee goes slamming over the counter. "You can take
those over hard up your ass, you little turd." And he throws the
sugar jar at the pass-through. We didn't figure it'd be a good
idea to wait around there to get our gas, so we tore back onto
the highway, this time I-40 East, toward the Roswell cut-off.

You know, sometimes I can really understand how Ellen felt.
Someone leaves you when you need their help, and all you
want is for them to show up. But even if they did come back,
they wouldn't stay, and that's the help you need. Yeah, I'm not
sure about that.

DOC (cont.)

We weren't fifteen minutes out when the twirling red lights were flashing behind us, and we had to pull over. "Well, cowboy, you sure speed along this highway like you own it, don't you? And you sure do throw a mean jar of sugar. Why don't you get out of the car now, mister?" I didn't move and Jim got out. I could pretty much hear, but in the dark, I couldn't clearly see what was happening.

"Hands up against the car. You sure are dumb, cowboy. I was having a danish just halfway down the counter when you pulled that stunt. Whoa, what have we here, a little weapon? Alright, let's go to my car."

And Jim says, "You don't need to jerk me around, I'll go."
"What was that Jesse James? What did you say to me?"
And he slams Jim against the side of the car. "I said leggo."
"You little cocksucker" Slam. "Jesus Shit" Slam. "Fuck you"
Slam. "Christ" "You're dead" Then I saw the cop had Jim by the head.

Have you ever done something so fast that it's over before you know it's started? I had the tire iron from under the front seat, an L-shaped sort of thing, out the door, onto the front hood, I used the outside rear-view mirror to get up there, started across, he saw me coming, pulled his gun, Jim lunged to the left and grabbed his arm then spun him around, the back of his head toward me and then my arm came around and there was a cracking sound that you've never ever heard before, even if you are a doctor. But as my momentum carried me to the ground and I rolled on the highway, I knew I had definitely knocked that guy over the fence. I got up and walked back to face our dead New Mexico Highway Patrolman.

56

Jim seemed lost, sitting there on the highway with a messy
dead man across his lap. I pulled the cop off him. I'd been
around enough dead people before, but they were always in
such clean surroundings. This guy had exploded. His pants
were full of shit, and his blood and brains were all over him.
He was so dead it seemed as though this was the only way he
ever existed, a completely nauseating and frightening sack of
garbage. My hands felt sticky for days.

Jim got in the car, turned it around, I picked the tire iron, got
in and we drove off without a word. Back through
Albuquerque and northwest on 44. I threw the tire iron out the
window somewhere near a town called Cuba. The idea was to
go through Four Corners into Utah. Who'd expect a couple of
cop-killers to go to Utah? And then maybe to Canada, but that
was undecided. The whole thing with the cop happened in a
grey, dead aired six a.m. That hour of the day seems to pop up
a lot with Jim and me, or at least did. Later that day as we
drove through northwest New Mexico, Jim began taking hits
off the warm bottle of gin and mumbling and battering the
steering wheel. After about a half hour of that he finally began
to talk to me.

"I'm so fucking sick of this. I've been standing up to, stood up
to, grabbed and been grabbed, defended myself and whatever I
had against every sort of rustler for so long and I finally
learned to poach off other people's lives and scramble for
whatever it was whether it was rightly mine or not, and there's
still no more elbow room than before, and you still got to
spend your time slapping and biting with every son of a bitch
who fancies something you got or doesn't like the way you
walk or wants the same job you do. Ever see this old movie

'The Misfits'? I bought the DVD for my wife - ex-wife - 'cause of the ti-le and she had always had a thing for Marilyn Monroe. But that fucking movie pissed me off. Parts of it were O.K., but in the end, it made a man feel ashamed if he had a goddamn job. I mean, shit, with this old-ass Clark Gable strutting around saying how he couldn't work for wages 'cause he's some kind of 'last of the cowboys' or some shit.

Hell, I work for wages. I've had hundreds of jobs, and I'm not ashamed of one of them, they just mostly didn't work out that's all. I'd sell light bulbs door to door if I could make any money at it. But that's it, nobody's allowed, period. And then some wide-eyed innocent comes walking in politely asking for some room if we all wouldn't mind and ends up popping the back end of a trooper's skull a country mile. It's always you fuckers who do the real damage. That's why I pulled you out of that bar back in Cheyenne.

That was your first bar fight wasn't it? And that dead weight back in New Mexico is your first big old notch in your fucking gun, isn't it? Who the fuck are you anyway? Some fucking clerk on vacation? I don't know why I don't let you out right here, you're just a trigger-happy kid, no matter how old you say you are. No, but you were going to save my life. How were you to know that he was just a cop who was going to bruise me up some, screw me for about a hundred dollars and send us on our way? No, you couldn't know that 'cause you don't know shit. Hey, you want to see something killer?"

He lifted up his shirt and there was this half-inch deep pock-mark, a deformed duplicate navel, on the right side of his stomach and he said, "I was looking for her. I knew they'd be together. I'd looked the other way for so long, I figured either she'd get over it or I would, a person can adjust, pain doesn't last forever. But one afternoon I was just sitting there watching TV when I started thinking about all the things we had said to each other when we were getting married, I actually believed that stuff, I did cherish, I did hold. I still do. I got enough beer in me, so I was crying and knocking shit around in the kitchen and I realized that it was her honor, my honor, and our marriage I had to protect. So, I grabbed the piece I had then, a thirty-eight, and drove into town looking for them. The second fucking stoplight in downtown Loveland, and there they were, in her fucking Volkswagen, on the opposite side of the street with the left turn signal flashing. Sherry, oh god Sherry, what's wrong with you?

And I'm yelling out the window, 'Get out of that fucking car you son of a bitch before I blow you sky high.' I was out of the car running towards them and he did get out but he had a gun too, but like a Glock or some nine millimeter shit he held two-handed like a cop, and before I could even stop he let go, and I was rolling in Main Street. I spent some time in the hospital and left town. It was ruled self-defense and he didn't press charges for assault."

Jim and I slept over in Montezuma creek, Utah in the Navajo Motel, and the next morning Jim said he'd been doing some thinking and he figured we'd better go to Canada, dump the car and split up there. First though, there was the Dinosaur Roundup Rodeo. If we stopped there, he figured he could make a few hundred dollars in winnings in two days, which would stake him some, and he'd give me a hundred when we got to Canada, so we headed toward Vernal.

DOC (cont.)

Utah is like one big Grand Canyon in the south there, with huge bluffs, and wind carved rocks. We wound through Moab, Crescent Junction, Green River, and took a right at Helper, Utah, where after a half day's driving on this little backwoods highway, we were getting into the mountains now, got us to Gusher, twenty-three miles south of Vernal, and the Cherokee runs out of gas. There is no gas to be had in Gusher, Utah on Sunday. One local guy offers to take us to Vernal and back for twenty dollars, Jim says screw that, we'll hitch, so we start walking out of town, along the highway, turning around whenever we hear a car coming.

We were just walking there, not saying much and I noticed what I was wearing and how authentic I looked. I was walking along looking at my faded torn-up jeans, and my beat-up boots, and I'd glance at the shadow of myself on the highway, the way my hat looked and all. It's the same stuff I have on now, but I couldn't help seeing myself do what I was doing. I was fascinated by my new life, new problems, new reasons, and the way I walked, talked, and thought. I wasn't a phony, I really was that person, or am, or who the hell knows. I do like my boots though, and the hat. I like everything.

Everything's fine. I especially like Utah, it's my home state now. I should start being a responsible citizen, get interested in politics, find out whether the Governor's a hard right or middle of the road Republican, find out who's the big cheese in the state legislature, and who knows, maybe get in a position of influence. I can at least be informed, vote responsibly, and learn the earthy mores of this picturesque southwestern state. maybe I'll become a Mormon and find out if God likes country music. And if he'll pay me to hum it and stare at the trees.

DOC (cont.)

Who says what is what, who really knows? Do you duck or run or shoot or shake hands or punch the fucking wise ass in the face? Who says, who knows, who even cares? But they sure as shit do care, even if it is in the most messed-up stupid back-assed way. They should issue cowboy guidebooks, like driver's manuals.

The dirty white Silverado crew cab pulled over in front of us about six pm, twelve hours opposite our favorite time, and three drunk cowboys crawl out. One starts pissing on the side of the road and the other two start walking toward us holding beers and slapping each other on the back. There was a lot of "Where you boys from, and have some beer, and where you headed?" And when we got back to their pickup it turns out that Jim knows the guy who was pissing, they fixed fence for the same guy once or something, and that's enough and they're going to take us to Vernal to get the gas and take us back to our car. Shit, yeah. Anything for an old working buddy.

I'm supposed to sit in the front seat with two guys and Frank. There's a shit load of laughter, and the pissing guy and Jim are sitting in the back with the big cooler of beer. I'm confused. I ask one of the guys I was squeezed between as we drove off if he was Frank. Haw-haw-haw everybody slapping their knees. The pissing guy is whispering to Jim and he laughs, then the guy on my right, who smells pretty damned bad, pushes aside a newspaper on the dashboard, this little head moved, and this whole thing sort of slid to the right in front of me. It was a fat brown rattlesnake. The snake's tongue flicks out like a lighter, just like in the movies. It stares at me and I turn to stone and break into a sweat, also just like in the movies. Boy, if you ever want to know what a cowboy thinks is funny, this is it.

DOC (cont.)

After they quiet down, the bad-smelling guy gets his hand on the back of my neck and starts squeezing it and telling me how tame the snake is, how they caught it in the desert by feeding it peanut butter, and pushes my face toward it, saying how I should get to know him better, the dashboard is his home, and he keeps their CD player from being ripped off and there's this, "Go on, get to know him, be his friend, say hello to Frank."

I learned in Cheyenne to do what a drunk cowboy tells you to do and to do it as sincerely as you know how. Well, the bad-smelling guy and everyone else was real satisfied with how I said hello. Even Jim said it was real satisfying.

Things got relatively quiet then, at least they ignored me, while I kept my eye on the snake and we drove into Vernal. If I had had any sense at all, I would have made some excuse at the gas station, going to the bathroom or something and taken off on my own, but instead I stayed sandwiched between the two guys in front while Jim and pissing guy bought a can of gas.

As we drove back toward Gusher, the guy on my left, the driver, started to talk to me saying how a man in this part of the country had to be real strong and have the right attitude towards his friends and didn't I think so. I said I didn't really know, and the bad-smelling guy says he's getting tired of my uppity untalkative ways. I didn't reply and then Jim knocks my hat off from behind me and says I'm just a dude from down south and it's about time I loosened up, got a little humble and took a lesson from those who were only trying to help me anyway. Well, then goddamn it alright but give me back my goddamn hat, but the driver has it smashed between his left side and the door and says I ain't gonna get shit unless I

DOC (cont.)

learn how to ask politely, at which Jim almost chokes to death
laughing, saying yeah ask him to apologize. He must have been
drinking a hell of a lot back there with the pissing guy, cause
he starts yelling for me to have a goddamn beer, and the
pissing guy starts hitting the back of my head to get me to turn
around, but I'm too scared to do anything now and the snake
is getting agitated. Alright! Alright! Whatever you say just let
me out of the goddamn truck let me out, let me out I'll go on
my own. Give me my hat and let me out of here.

And the truck veers to the right and pulls to a full stop off the
shoulder. The driver tells me I could've gotten us all killed and
I gotta learn a little patience and not to go screaming around
like some kind of pussy. Then we're all out of the truck and
Bad Smell has got me by the arm and says he wants to show
me something that might do me some good and we're at the
tailgate and Pissing Guy pulls it down and grabs this half-sized
Styrofoam cooler wedged back there and shoves it toward me.
Bad Smell tells me that old Frank in the front seat is a nice guy
cause he's old, and if he bit you, you'd have about an hour to
get to the hospital before you died, but on the other hand, if
little Frank bites you, you got less than five minutes before you
start to feel it and you're dead in ten. Young ones are far more
deadly. He's got my hand held against the edge of the cooler,
holding me by the wrist, and he says he wants me to apologize
to everyone, including big and little Frank and promise that I'll
get off my high horse and be more respectful. And Jesus I
can't, and somehow with my free hand I throw the cooler at
Bad smell's face, he yells, the snake is out, on someone? I don't
know and the driver's there he hits me, and I hit him, I get my
hat, I start to run then everything's quiet, and Jim's got me by
my wrists and telling me to calm down in that super low voice

63

DOC (cont.)

he uses when he's about to tear someone up. Now, I don't know if you've ever had your wrists held up to your face like that, but it's pretty near impossible to keep calm. He calls me trigger happy again and I scream, "Fuck you – leggo!" And I kick and kick and I'm free but then I'm not and I see that pearl handle steel and Jim's face all screwed up, and Jesus, I didn't steal his fucking wife.

I woke up with the back of my head a big throbbing lump and everything hurting, but they did leave me my hat. Sheriff says local boys told him that they had helped a cowboy subdue me after I'd forced him at gunpoint - there was a single shot Colt .22 pistol left as evidence - to drive me up north, trying to get to Canada. Seems that this cowboy, named Jim, had picked me up hitching, and I had told him all about killing a highway patrolman who had stopped me from hitching, it's illegal in New Mexico, and I had whacked him with a tire iron that I carried in my satchel for self-defense.

Cowboy said I was drunk when I told him all this. The sheriff didn't flinch at the implausibility of the whole story because cowboy Jim had left before he had a chance to talk to him directly, it was all second hand, but they were going to check down in Cuba, New Mexico anyway for the tire iron that I ditched without even bothering to wipe it off. Or so he was told. They found it. They'll never find Jim. They won't even look for him, because I told them that they had me dead to rights and who gives a shit anyway.

DOC, his voice soft and haunted, sings.

DOC (cont.)
And I'd pawn you my gold watch and chain love and I'd pawn you my gold wedding ring
And I'd pawn you this heart in my bosom only say that you'll love me again
The white rose that blooms in the garden it blooms with this love in my heart
It broke through on the day that I met you it will die on the day that we part

I've lost almost any connection with my past I may have had. One thing for sure though. There's no such thing as betrayal, there's only hit and run. "There are some things a doctor can do nothing about." That's old Doc Simpson talking. He's probably out mowing his lawn or taking somebody's pulse right now. "Sometimes you'll see a patient and the only thing they have is their disease."

LIGHTING CHANGE reveals the stairway behind the back wall. He crosses UPSTAGE RIGHT opens the door and heads up.

"Everything else is eaten away. All you do is take care of the pain and hand them over. Don't fight for a lost cause - just step out of the way." I wonder if he ever got around to digging up his driveway to plant that vegetable garden.

DOC'S legs crash through the open shaft in the ceiling. He's hung, his boots swing in the dusty shaft of light.

LIGHTS FADE

CURTAIN

Production Notes

The sets and lighting for both plays as described are based on the set designs by John Kavelin and lighting by Barbara Ling, in collaboration with Robert Altman for both the Los Angeles Actors Theatre and the Off-Broadway St. Clements Theater productions. The actors' stage directions as written, are derived from Robert Altman's direction.

The actors in these original professional productions, Alfre Woodard, Cliff DeYoung, Guy Boyd, and Leo Burmester, as well as James Horan in many independent performances of *Rattlesnake in a Cooler*, taught me much about the emotional life and motivation of the characters they brought to life on stage. I incorporated what I learned from them in rewrites during rehearsals and after performances.

Though both plays benefited immeasurably from the above contributions, they are open for original interpretation by actors, directors, set and lighting designers.

I hope the publication of *2 by South* makes it possible for others to be inspired to bring *Rattlesnake in a Cooler* and *Precious Blood* to new life.

PERFORMANCE HISTORY

Rattlesnake in a Cooler   October 9–20, 1980
626 Broadway NYC
Produced by Interaction Arts Foundation
Cast – Frank South
Set by Joseph Lowery
Directed by Joseph Lowey and Frank South

Precious Blood   March 13-22, 1981
626 Broadway NYC
Produced by Interaction Arts Foundation
Cast – Debra Wanner and Frank South

Precious Blood   May 1981
University of Georgia, Athens GA
Produced by Interaction Arts
Cast – Debra Wanner and Frank South

2 by South   June 10 – August 2, 1981
Los Angeles Actors Theatre
Produced by Diane White, Bill Bushnell
Cast – Alfre Woodard, Cliff DeYoung, Leo Burmester, Danny Darst
Scenery by John Kavelin, Lights by Barbara Ling
Directed by Robert Altman

2 by South   October 6 – December 7, 1981
St Clement's Theatre, Off-Broadway NYC
Produced by M.G.I. and Scott Bushnell
Cast - Alfre Woodard, Guy Boyd, Leo Burmester, Danny Darst
Scenery by John Kavelin, Lights by Barbara Ling
Directed by Robert Altman

2 by South   January 14 – March 6, 1983
Detroit Repertory Theatre, Detroit MI
Cast – Paul E Scheier, Fran L Washington, Council Cargle,
Dee Andrus, Monica Sobierai, William Boswell, Darius Dudley
Sets by Bruce Millan, Lights by Marylynn Kacir, Steve Dambach
Directed by Bruce Millan

Rattlesnake in a Cooler   April 15 – May 6, 1983
Bailiwick Repertory, Chicago, IL
Cast - Matt DeCaro and Neil Flynn
Directed by Doug Finlayson

Rattlesnake in a Cooler   September 19 – 28, 1991
Stages Theater Complex, Hollywood, CA
Cast – Joe Deese
Directed by Blanche Sindelar

Rattlesnake in a Cooler   June 17, 1994
The Ventura Court Theatre, Studio City, CA
Cast – James Horan
Directed by Ayers Baxter

Rattlesnake in a Cooler   1995
Camilla's Theatre Gallery, SoHo, NYC
Cast - James Horan
Directed by Ayers Baxter

Rattlesnake in a Cooler   1998
LA Theatre Center, Los Angeles, CA
Cast – James Horan
Directed by Ayers Baxter

Rattlesnake in a Cooler   August 17, 2001 / Sept 6 – 8, 2002
Celtic Arts Center, LA CA
Cast – James Horan
Directed by Ayers Baxter

Rattlesnake in a Cooler   June 27, 2009
Lake Carmel Arts Center, Kent Lakes NY
Cast - Daniel Burmester
Directed by Jonathan Maloney & Kali Quinn
Produced by GUTworks Theatre Co.

Rattlesnake in a Cooler   July 8–9, 2009
Hooker Dunham Theatre, Brattleboro VT
Cast - Daniel Burmester
Directed by Jonathan Maloney & Kali Quinn
Produced by GUTworks Theatre Co.

Rattlesnake in a Cooler   January 27 – 28, 2012
South of Broadway, Charleston, South Carolina
Cast – James Horan

Rattlesnake in a Cooler   May 6 – 12, 2019
Irish Import Shop, Hollywood, CA
Cast – James Horan

*History is not ensured to be accurate or comprehensive.

PHOTOS

626 / Interaction Arts / NoHo, NYC

Precious Blood

Frank South and Debra Wanner

photos: Marty Heitner

Rattlesnake in a Cooler

Frank South

Rattlesnake in a Cooler – Joe Lowery's Enveloping Set Design

1) Play begins - conduit/rope tepees, 3 10 ft wooden poles w/eyebolts on floor, bed, rope anchors in wall, ropes through ceiling pulleys.

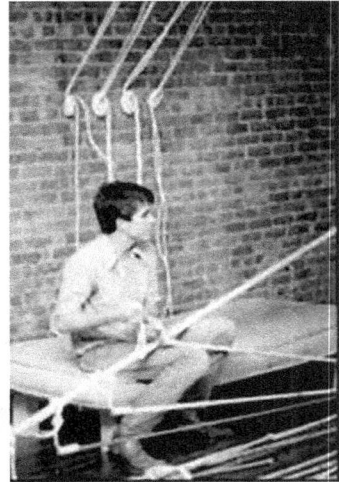

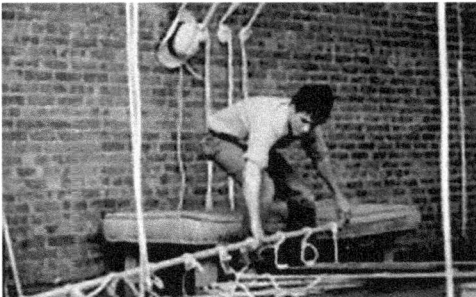

2) While performing play, take conduit pieces from teepees and tie to poles.

3) As play progresses drag each pole with attached conduit behind, then the next two beside audience, clipping them to hanging ropes from ceiling pulleys, all the time performing the play.

Photos: Marty Heitner

4) Play ends with last line from Doc as he pulls the poles and conduit clanging to the ceiling putting the audience with him in the cell of his making - limited the audience size some, but worth it.

Los Angeles Actors Theater – 2 by South

Precious Blood

Cliff DeYoung and Alfre Woodard

Photos: Richard S. Bailey

Rattlesnake in a Cooler

Leo Burmester and Danny Darst

Los Angeles Actors Theater – 2 by South

Robert Altman - publicity shot for *2 by South* LAAT premier.

Photo: Richard S. Bailey

St. Clements Theater, Off-Broadway – 2 by South

Precious Blood

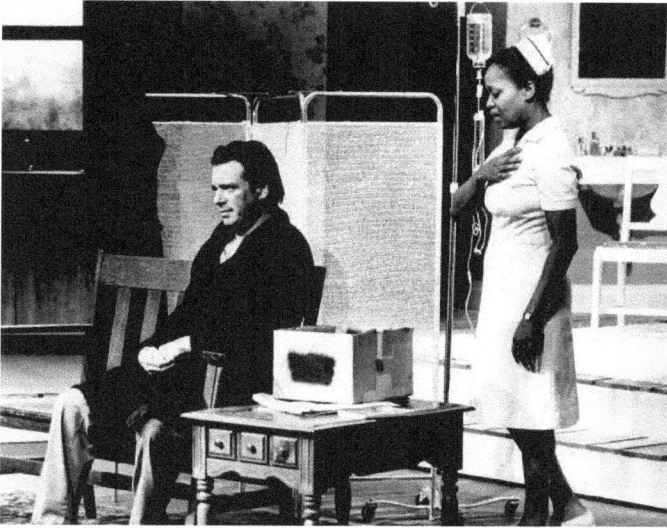

Guy Boyd and Alfre Woodard

Photos: Joan Pagliuso

Alfre Woodard

St. Clements Theater, Off-Broadway – 2 by South

Rattlesnake in a Cooler

Leo Burmester

Photos: Joan Pagliuso

Leo Burmester

ABC Arts Cable TV

Two people fatefully caught in the grip of their own tragic past.

Alfre Woodard

Precious Blood

Directed by: Robert Altman

abc

Leo Burmester

A young man's life of promise turns to tragedy on a lonely New Mexico highway.

Rattlesnake in a Cooler

Directed by: Robert Altman

abc

77

Detroit Repertory Theatre, Detroit MI
Rattlesnake in a Cooler

Council Cargle   photo: Bruce Millan

Lake Carmel Arts Center, Kent Lakes NY
Rattlesnake in a Cooler

Daniel Burmester

photo courtesy of Jonathan Maloney & Kali Quinn

Camilla's Theatre Gallery, NYC
Rattlesnake in a Cooler

James Horan
Photo: Ayers Baxter

South of Broadway, Charleston, SC
Rattlesnake in a Cooler

James Horan
photo: Mark Gorman

American Film Institute, Rattlesnake Screening

ABC VIDEO ENTERPRISES, INC.
AND THE AMERICAN FILM INSTITUTE
HONOR

ROBERT ALTMAN

MARCH 9, 1982

"I believe a new style is evolving in the dramatic arts, a style calling for an even greater intimacy and contact between audience and performer than is possible in the theater or in movies. Such a style may well find its ultimate expression in cable television." —Robert Altman

Robert Altman and
Robert Reed Altman
shooting *2 by South*

Frank South, Altman & Herbert Granath; by James A. Parcell—The Washington Post

ACKNOWLEDGEMENTS

Joseph Lowery, Debra Wanner, and Bill Gordh of Interaction Arts provided the inspiration, guidance, ideas, and labor that brought both plays to life for the first time at 626 Broadway. Their talent and continued friendship made it possible for the plays and for me to succeed.

The brave women and men who told me their personal stories during the writing of *Precious Blood* educated and humbled me. I hope I served you well.

Warm thanks to my first agent, Steven Dansky for his tireless energy and patience. When Steven gave Leo Burmester *Rattlesnake in a Cooler,* Leo took it to Bob Altman, and it all took off from there. I miss Leo's originality and wild enthusiasm. Leo introduced me to Danny Darst's poetry and music that, along with Danny's performance, added depth and resonance to the Los Angeles Actors' Theatre and St. Clements Theatre productions.

Bob and Kathryn Altman opened their home to me in Los Angeles and New York. Kathryn was gracious and kind from the outset and stayed so throughout the years. I owe Bob Altman a great deal. I was fortunate to work and learn from his uncompromising vision and artistry, directly and by example. He was a giant talent and a generous, inspiring friend.

www.ingramcontent.com/pod-product-compliance
Lightning Source LLC
Chambersburg PA
CBHW031524040426
42445CB00009B/381